Contents

Acknowledgements

This publication has been made possible through the generosity of the Public Library Improvement Fund, administered by the Scottish Library & Information Council. The content originated as a war centenary exhibition at the Shetland Museum and Archives, and special thanks are due to those whose work made that show a success, above all Nina Goodlad and John Hunter, and Lerwick Port Authority for its financial support. The following kindly provided specific photographs: Margaret Halcrow, Eddie Knight, Nic Paton, Felicity Podger, Margaret Stuart; Steven Christie and Davy Cooper undertook scanning and photography. Besides donors of the past, thanks go to those who gifted items especially for the show: Davie Anderson, Hazel Hughson, Charlie Simpson, Les Smith, and special thanks go to the National Fund for Acquisitions, especially Hazel Williamson.

The tide of war

The centenary of the First World War is upon us, and people everywhere are examining the way their own communities were drawn into that cataclysm. The story of a war is composed of countless small tales, but there is a danger that national experiences eclipse local ones, and certain aspects of the onslaught are forgotten, because people find it too obscure today. By far the largest historical casualty is the role of Britain's seaborne war: mention the war to most folk, and they'd think of trenches, barbed wire, and poison gas. This is particularly regrettable for Shetland, for ours was a markedly maritime conflict, and applying national experiences, often best applicable to urban communities, doesn't match distinctive trends in our own war. For all that millions of Britons served in the Army, the nation's main strategic strength was its Navy, not its land forces, and the Allies would stand or fall on their ability to control the oceans and the flow of materiel to the western front. The facts that made this achievable are incomprehensible for us today: our empire, merchant fleet and navy were the world's largest.

This had special resonance in Shetland, where 70% on war service were sailors or merchant seamen. During the war's voracious appetite for manpower, troopships leaving Lerwick with reserve contingents carried many more sailors than soldiers, and all the while merchant seamen continued their peacetime trade. In summer 1915 Shetland's 250 army reservists left Lerwick, but this figure is dwarfed by the number of men who enrolled in the naval reserve; besides 450 mobilised in 1914, 250 more left in 1915, and then 700 during 1916. Only conscription and colonial enlistment later boosted the Army ratio, but the sea services still dominated all the same.

On course to fight

Fighting on land was only secure when another element was controlled firmly, and people once talked of seapower as one would speak of airpower today. Britain's global trading reach necessitated a huge navy. Germany's own fleet, expanded from 1890s, was intended to be a potent deterrent, rather than a stage in eclipsing Britain, but the latter responded by modernising and expanding her own navy. The press and public commentary were dominated by the issue of the naval arms race and the challenge to the balance of power. On the outbreak of war, the greatest strategic asset Britain possessed was her stupendous Naval strength, which brought a seemingly invincible advantage to the Allies' cause. Although other nations' navies contributed to that effort, it was the British navy that ensured troops could be ferried largely without mishap throughout the war, and even in the face of a devastating German naval campaign by submarines in 1917, the nation's survival was ensured. The greatest strategic threat Germany faced was the British navy, which had the power to cut off her maritime trade, its link between its empire and countries where vital imports came from. This was a main factor driving her strategists towards a fast victory: the more protracted the conflict, the more dangerous the country's situation would be (Strachan 2003:44). Germany's geopolitical challenge was its reliance on neutral shipping to import commodities vital for the nation's survival, because Britain had swept all German shipping off the oceans by autumn 1914. Sailors and the public in Britain hoped for a clash of war fleets as soon as the war broke, which promised to be a crushing victory. However, the war didn't run nicely to plan, and tactics had to abandoned in the face of minefields and submarines, and economic warfare. Trade and diplomacy shaped the war, as war prices for shipment soared, vessels from European neutral nations transported lucrative shipments from the United States, who, in turn, resented any interference with business as usual. The diplomatic niceties in gaining, and boosting, sympathy for the Allies were tricky.

The call to duty

What, then, of Shetland's own war experience? Our perception is especially dominated by the imagery of bloodshed in horrific trench warfare and pitifully vast war cemeteries. Dreadful though this was, it also ignores much. Firstly, most people weren't in the armed forces at all, but the war affected them too. Secondly, most Shetlanders in the services served at sea, not in the Army. Thirdly, most servicemen weren't casualties at all, and those who were mostly endured wounds, not death. This is not to downplay the appalling carnage, but it is, instead, a chance to rebalance the view of how war touched both Shetland and Shetlanders.

The makeup of society shaped the kind of war we experienced, for islanders were a rural people and men earned their living afloat, with incomes from fishing or going to sea supporting families at home. All the while, women ran the family farms for much of year while men were away, undertaking work with livestock and crops, as well as household and childrearing duties. Their work meant the islands coped remarkably well with the dislocation when war came, and the men's peacetime vocation ensured Shetland's war was an overwhelmingly maritime one. Hundreds of seamen and fishermen were members of the Royal Naval Reserve, so were mobilised in 1914, and in the volunteering fervour that continued into 1916, it was the Navy that benefited from Shetlanders' patriotism.

Shetland's strategic role

The title of this volume is just a little whimsical. Whatever the nature of islanders' war, Shetland's contribution was similar to every county, in that it was a source of manpower. But in a special way the islands (as opposed to the people) played a far more crucial role in the war – of international strategic stature.

The Allies couldn't win the war by combat alone, and a crucial aim was to wreck their enemies' economy. Germany needed supplies from across the Atlantic, but the British Navy had cleared its ships from the oceans, so the Germans used ships from non-combatant countries to carry their goods instead. Because of its geographical position, Shetland was indispensable to this, the longest campaign of the war. The blockade aimed to stop German trade, confiscating anything bound there, for a rigid blockade would deprive the enemy of supplies to clothe, transport, equip and feed its war machine, and thereby fatally weaken the nation. Neutral trade was legitimate, but in the desperate conditions of war Britain declared many materials contraband to imply shipping companies were smuggling. Shipping firms ran huge risks, but made big profits too; war was psychological, and lucrative. Unratified convention considered commodities "absolute contraband", "conditional contraband", or "free list". The system was unworkable, for foodstuffs and oil were only contraband if intended for warlike intentions, and anything going to neutral ports was exempt. These nuances were easy to evade. Furthermore, German agents were resourceful in obscuring the paper trail, so as the war intensified Britain often unilaterally changed the rules, expanding the range of raw materials it confiscated, such as cotton.

Merchants of war

The Admiralty formed the 10th Cruiser Squadron to implement the blockade. Regular warships were used at first, accompanied by a few armed liners. The cruisers couldn't cope with furious storms and encountered engine breakdowns, so in December 1914 the squadron was replaced by twenty-four armed merchant cruisers, crewed by 9,800 men. The reformed 10th C.S. was comprised of converted liners, because they were economical on coal, could cover long distances, and could withstand tempests. Conversion involved dismantling all inflammable fixtures and state rooms, changing cabins to berths, erecting magazines, removing derricks and skylights, mounting guns and searchlights, installing gunnery control, and loading extra ballast. The squadron patrolled the North Atlantic, on the lookout for ships day and night, challenging all it found. A typical patrol consisted of half a dozen vessels spaced at 15 mile intervals, turning every two hours diurnally, and every three hours nocturnally, keeping a cruising speed of 9-10 knots, because greater speed was wasteful of fuel.

When a cruiser spotted a merchant ship, it was ordered to stop by signal, and a boarding party was prepared. Lowering the boat was hazardous, as it was winched down from a derrick, allowing it to catch the swell the instant it touched the water. The sailors searched the neutral ship, and Naval reservists who were seamen before the war had the knowledge to find places of concealment in the engineroom, stokehold, or lockers. Interception and investigation hampered the ship's trade, but only if the mercantile skipper refused to comply did the British officer take direct charge; the most argumentative and least biddable officers were Americans. The boarding party directed the ship to Lerwick, where a more thorough investigation of the ship continued and if any cargo was deemed contraband, the neutral was sent to a mainland British port to offload, and the government seized the goods.

The British viewed themselves as protecting trade, albeit in Allied interests, and their merchant cruisers were a defensive force. The German navy used armed merchants too, but to attack maritime trade. They were disguised as neutral merchant vessels, and had hidden weaponry that they deployed on their quarry. All these German merchant cruisers had to evade the 10th Cruiser Squadron to get to the open oceans, and some engaged in fierce fights with their British equivalents. The British government put two of the cruisers under nominal French control in spring 1915 to give the notion that it was an Allied effort, but the French didn't excel, dragging their anchors, pretending not to see ships' lights at night, and declaring that it was too rough to board vessels in conditions that British-crewed vessels managed. The ships were later rescinded.

Shetlanders in the big fight

Around a hundred Shetlanders were involved in the blockade in some way, whether on armed liners, armoured cruisers, boarding steamers, minesweepers, colliers, or other craft. For most, their route was through the Royal Naval Reserve. Willie Mann (Bouster, Yell) was a seaman, and as war rumours were rife in August 1914, his crewmates discussed the news as their ship departed to Cardiff to load a cargo of coal. There, reservists got passes for the Devonport barracks, where Willie was informed he'd be joining H.M.S. *Oceanic* once she arrived from New York. Willie was supplied with a uniform, and after a week he was with his ship, on the 10th Cruiser Squadron (Mann 1966:5). Another mariner, John Hoseason (Camb, Yell) paid-off from his ship in August 1914, and had to report to the Devonport base, where it was so crowded he slept his first night under the mess table, having eaten nothing all day. Issued with kit, he received field training and heavy gun drill, before being assigned a ship. In 1915 he was promoted to Sub-Lieutenant, and spent a gunnery command course at Portsmouth, before being appointed to H.M.S. *Ambrose*, in the 10th C.S. (Hoseason 1954). James Morrison (Bigton, Dunrossness) went to the recruiting office at the Lerwick fishmarket to enlist, and was asked if he was a fisherman; "That was all the qualification needed. Passing the doctor didn't take many minutes". James was sent onto H.M.S. *Brilliant*, where he was kitted-out with uniform and told to report back to the recruiting office. There, his group of ratings boarded a lorry to Busta. He was sent to H.M.S. *Gibraltar*, where there were hundreds of men quartered, mostly stokers from the 10th Cruiser Squadron. After some days, James's name was called and he was allocated to H.M.T. *Hondo*, a patrol trawler protecting Swarbacks Minn (Morrison 1992:10).

Atlantic supply base

The ships of the 10th C.S. were on patrol for two weeks, spent two or three days at Bustavoe for resupply, then every three months the vessel went to either Glasgow or Liverpool docks for heavy maintenance for around a week and a half. Bressay Sound and Bustavoe were adopted as bases in August 1914. The blockade was strengthened by the 2nd Cruiser Squadron that intercepted neutral ships trying to evade the blockade by going far north, and near the Norwegian coast. This unit comprised regular Navy cruisers, and converted fast passenger ships. The facilities at Lerwick catered for the 10th C.S.'s huge examination duties, and administration. The scale of work exceeded anything in peacetime. For example, from July to September 1916 alone 269 vessels were examined at Lerwick; "the fine spectacle of seven full rigged sailing ships at one time in the harbour being a memorable one to all lovers of the sea", and in one year 150 persons deemed of suspect enemy nationality were removed and detained from vessels under examination at Lerwick (*Shetland News* 1919). Bustavoe was the supply base, but the district was a typical rural setting, with no infrastructure to cater for shipping. By spring 1915 the Admiralty had built an impressive network at Bustavoe, catering for coaling, food supply, crew changes, medical care, and recreation. Moorings were laid, navigational markers erected, and shipping companies were chartered to send ships with supplies of coal, food, and equipment. Coaling was hugely labour-intensive, coal being loaded into baskets lowered to the collier, where they were filled, then hoisted aboard the Navy ship. Baskets were tipped in the bunkers, then trimmers and stokers shifted the load. Cruisers usually took two days to re-bunker, and, depending on the size of vessel, took on around 1,500 tons. Vessels required water for their crew and the ship's boilers; it was pumped onboard water tenders which delivered the water to the ships directly.

The blockade ships' presence made Bustavoe a prime target, and a powerful gun battery protected the Swarbacks Minn entrance of the base, with two ship's guns, a lookout station, and crews were billeted at Uyeasound and Vementry. The main threat was enemy submarines, so anti-submarine nets were installed at Bustavoe and Bressay Sound. These were held in tension by anchors and buoys, and were opened by trawlers winching a hinged opening that allowed vessels to pass in or out. Ships regularly entered or left in darkness, to avoid submarine attack. The trawlers on Navy service kept six hours on and six hours off. The patrol trawler challenged any vessel it encountered approaching the base. The trawler closed the distance, then signalled a challenge message by flag or lamp.

When a vessel was coming in, the patrol boat made full speed for the boom defence, blowing her whistle to signal the boom defence vessel to open the net. Besides British defensive minefields, German submarines laid mines along the northwest approaches to Shetland, flanking the 10th C.S.'s base, and the east side, endangering Lerwick. To counteract this, minesweepers maintained swept channels through the minefields. Boats worked in pairs, towing a cable with cutters which severed the wires holding the submerged mines in place below the surface, and the surfaced mine was sunk by the boat's deck gun.

The hundreds of personnel coming ashore on shore leave offered the opportunity for local folk to trade with the sailors, who bought farm produce as a welcome respite from ships' rations. Shetland's rural society offered little to crewmen seeking the excitement of sea ports, so the few shops and licensed premises in the blockade base district did very well. In fact, the local people were beneficiaries, as they attended music, sport, and drama events laid-on by the sailors themselves, and it was an exciting time to be a child, with the movements of shipping and vehicles plus a bumper harvest of flotsam to be investigated; prize items were hats with cap-bands with name tallies of merchant cruisers.

The critical year

Events in 1917 were decisive for the Allied cause. Germany inaugurated the campaign of sinking all shipping in the seas around Britain, bringing devastating losses to merchant shipping, and Russia withdrew from the war. However, the U.S.A. entered the war on the Allied side, and its industrial capabilities were able to build ships faster than Germany could sink them, and now all grain from North America was Allied property. The balance tilted the next year irrevocably in the Allies' favour. In Shetland, 1917 saw the centre of gravity shift massively to Bressay Sound, when the convoy system was instituted in March that year. This had been urged by the Mercantile Marine for years, but the Admiralty had been intransigent, and only now it finally saw sense. Additionally, now that the United States was an ally, control of cargoes was possible at source, so interception at sea was not necessary. By grouping warship escorts around an assembly of merchant vessels, defensive resources and merchant ships were concentrated in a group that was risky to attack. Lerwick became the Allies' convoy port, and Shetland maintained its monumental importance to Allied strategy. Vessels waiting for departure in Britain steamed to Bressay Sound, where they gathered into a convoy, and destroyers and armed trawlers escorted it across the German Ocean. During 1917 4,500 vessels used Bressay Sound, and the tonnage passing through Lerwick was reputed to be greater than any other port in the kingdom. The largest number of vessels at Lerwick harbour at one time was on 23 Sep. 1917, with 79 warships, and 60 merchant vessels (*Shetland News* 1919). This needed impressive organisation, and in 1917 the Admiralty founded the Lerwick

Sub-Division of the Women's Royal Naval Service, based at Harbour Street. Gun emplacements protecting both entrances of Bressay Sound were erected in 1918.

Cause and effect

Were it not for the British navy, the Allies' war would have been lost. The outcome of the war was decided on the battlefields of France and Belgium, especially the flow of troops from Britain and her empire, and later the American army entering the scene. The safety of all these movements was overwhelmingly dependant on our navy; it ensured the flow of troops, munitions, food, supplies, vehicles, horses and fodder, over the English Channel and the Atlantic. British naval might meant Germany couldn't deploy its own formidable navy to attack the Allies. By spring 1917 the blockade "was beginning to inflict real damage at a moment when inflation, harvest failure, and over-expenditure on armaments were pushing the German economy into crisis" (Stevenson 2005:250). Blockade was a principal Allied strategy, but the 10th Cruiser Squadron was not singularly instrumental in causing their enemies' economic collapse, because the central powers were flanked by enemies on all fronts, so blockade was also imposed on the continent. Of course there were many reasons for victory, but it is gainful to speculate on the outcome had there been no maritime blockade. As military historian Julian Thomson makes clear, the "German war effort would have been unimpeded. The Germans would not have had to resort to unrestricted submarine warfare, and it follows that the United States would have very likely not joined the Allied side" (Thompson 2005:172-173). In that instance, the events of summer 1918 on the Western Front would have had a very different outcome. An unexpected place for a naval defeat.

References

Hoseason, J. "My Life at Sea, Including Two World Wars", *Shetland News* 9 Nov. 1954
Mann, W. "The wreck of the Oceanic", *New Shetlander* 77, 1966
Morrison, J. "Fishermen at War" pt. 1, *New Shetlander* 181, 1992
Shetland News "Lerwick Naval Base. Some Further Details", 18 Dec. 1919
Stevenson, D. *1914-1918*, London 2005
Strachan, H. *The First World War*, London 2003
Thompson, J. *War at Sea 1914-18*, London 2005

What do you associate with the First World War – soldiers, trenches and barbed wire? A hundred years after the conflict, we should remember the war touched everyone, civilians included, and Britain's main strength was its Navy, not the Army.

Nowhere showed this better than Shetland, where 70% on war service were sailors or merchant seamen. The islands themselves, not the islanders, were more important for the Allies, because we played a strategic role in the international struggle.

Britain's mighty blockade brought a sudden change, and Shetland hosted anchorages, coaling, anti-submarine defences and minesweeping. Locals experienced a buzz in social life, and trading took off. The Allies' war was Shetland's war.

Entrance
Swarbacks Minn – the narrowest
point between Vementry and
Muckle Roe. It was protected
by three anti-submarine nets,
gun defences, and a minefield:
getting in wasn't straightforward
even for our own Navy

tre of activity
tavoe, looking
evdaness, near
hersta. This was
anchorage for
chant cruisers,
royers, trawlers,
dozens more craft
any types.

The crossroads
The waters around Linga and the entrance to Olnafirth was very busy, where ships
coming in for coal or supplies, or destroyers and minesweepers leaving on patrol,
had to pass. It was a skilful piece of planning to keep all this running smoothly.

All at sea

Warships at anchor
A submarine, boarding
steamer, tug and
other warships in the
Sound at Lerwick.

Destroyer force
A flotilla of destroyers was always on station
at Lerwick, to escort merchant ship convoys.

St Nicholas at Swarbacks Minn
The regular civilian steamer service continued in wartime. The *St Nicholas* is passing between Muckle Roe and Vementry.

Warships in the Sound
Oilers, merchant cruiser, and other Navy craft anchored in Bressay Sound. The north half of the fishmarket was the 10th Cruiser Squadron's examination office.

Peacetime Shetland society shaped its wartime experience. Men made income as fishermen or merchant seamen, so this meant women shouldered most work on the land while the wage-earners were afloat.

Hundreds of men earned extra money by serving as Naval reservists. They were liable to be mobilised into full-time service if war broke out, which was what happened in 1914. Thousands of men were away in the war, so women continued as in peacetime, plus taking on voluntary war work.

The Royal Naval Reserve comprised experienced mariners who did part-time naval training. Not all seamen were in it, and hundreds more continued their work on merchant ships during the war. Like elsewhere, people played a role at home or overseas, as servicemen or civilians; most Shetlanders were civilians, working the land or fishing, or merchant seamen. Able-bodied men who weren't at sea were in the armed forces.

Who keeps Shetland going?
With so many men working afloat, the farm work fell to older folk, children and – most of all – the women. This meant Shetland was uniquely able to cope with the strain when war came.

Wages from the sea
Thousands of Shetlanders worked as fishermen or merchant seamen; their wages improved the family life of islanders. Around half were also Navy reservists, bringing in more income.

What we did in the Great War

Stationed at the base
Sailors of the Royal Naval Reserve,
Shetland Section, at the Busta barracks.

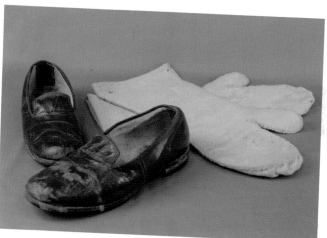

Slippers and mittens
Weisdale; Cunningsburgh |
1914-1918
Gunners wore safety gear in the
gun turrets and ammunition
stores. The Navy issue slippers
belonged to Jeemie Arthur,
Stromfirth, who wore them in
the shifting room. The gunner's
mittens belonged to Malcolm
Smith, Aith, who was a gunner
on the armed merchant cruiser
H.M.S. *Orbita*.
*Donated by Robbie Arthur,
Stromfirth; Douglas Smith,
Cunningsburgh | APP 2008.58;
SEA 2014.83*

First-aid book, identity disc
Delting; Foula | 1914-1918
The manual belonged to William
Comloquoy who was from Orkney and
stayed at Gonfirth. The disc belonged
to Peter Manson, Blobersburn.
*Donated by Harry Stevenson,
Lerwick; Leslie Manson, Kirkcaldy |
MIL 2005.32; WAR 1993.380*

Busta telephonists
Other than the officers, most of the sailors at the blockade base were Shetlanders. All but
one of the telephonists were locals: Back; Horne, Irvine. Front; Coutts, Arthur, McGregor.

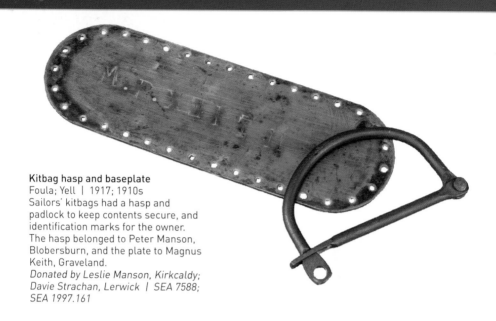

Kitbag hasp and baseplate
Foula; Yell | 1917; 1910s
Sailors' kitbags had a hasp and
padlock to keep contents secure, and
identification marks for the owner.
The hasp belonged to Peter Manson,
Blobersburn, and the plate to Magnus
Keith, Graveland.
Donated by Leslie Manson, Kirkcaldy;
Davie Strachan, Lerwick | SEA 7588;
SEA 1997.161

Hatbox, collar, necktie, stamp
Cunningsburgh | 1914
Everything in the Navy
carried identification marks.
Each sailor had an ink
stamp to print his name on
all garments. These items
belonged to Charlie Tulloch,
Wilhoul, crewman on the
merchant cruiser *Columbella*.
Donated by Charlie Simpson,
Cunningsburgh | WAR
2014.346; WAR 2014.347

Tunic, hat, knife
Cunnasting; Burra; Whalsay | 1910s
Shetland naval reservists' kit items:
the tunic belonged to John Johnson
(Kirkabister), the hat to John Smith
(Houss), and the knife to John
Stewart (Sandwick).
*Donated by Rhoda Bulter, Lerwick;
Barbara Sandison, Lerwick; John
Jamieson, Whalsay | SEA 1995.297;
WAR 2008.91; WAR 1998.127*

Picture frame
Sandwick | 1917-1918
Hobbies filled many an hour onboard
warships. William Smith, Milton, made
this frame from "Players" cigarette
packets while serving on the battleship
H.M.S. *Resolution*. His photo is in the
centre.
*Donated by Martin Smith, Lerwick |
WAR 2006.94*

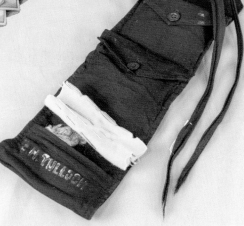

Sewing kit
Cunningsburgh | 1914
Every sailor had a Navy-issue
kit for running repairs to his
uniform. This one was used
in the 10th Cruiser Squadron
by Charlie Tulloch, Wilhoul,
onboard H.M.S. *Columbella*.
*Donated by Hazel Hughson,
Cunningsburgh | WAR 2015.4*

Cutting the supply line

The Allies couldn't win the war by combat alone, and
a crucial aim was to wreck their enemies' economy.
Germany needed supplies from across the Atlantic,
but the British Navy had cleared its ships from the
oceans, so the Germans used ships from countries not
fighting in the war to carry their goods instead. Britain's
blockade was all about stopping these neutrals, and
confiscating anything bound for its foe.

The blockade meant Germany couldn't get supplies
to clothe, transport, equip and feed its war machine.
This would fatally weaken the nation. The 10th Cruiser
Squadron enforced this operation, and Shetland was at
the forefront because the unit's forward base was in the
islands.

Neutral trade was legitimate, but Britain declared many
materials "contraband" to imply shipping companies
were smuggling. Neutral firms ran huge risks, but
made big profits too; war was psychological, and
lucrative.

Shutting-in the enemy
Britain knew it could use its vast navy to block-off the North Sea and stop the Germans getting out. By basing the navy in the Northern Isles there was less danger to our navy, but it would take a long time to starve the enemy of supplies. The public wanted a big battle, but blockades didn't work like that, and the war took four years.

The first of many
The first neutral sailing vessel brought to Lerwick by the 10th Cruiser Squadron was the Norwegian *Nordsie*.

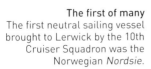

Cutting the supply line

Examination at Lerwick
Norwegian ship *Transatlantic*,
brought into Lerwick harbour for
examination for war contraband.

Empty the hold
The Swedish ship *Hispania*, carrying a cargo of fruit and other goods, was stopped by the 10th Cruiser Squadron and sent to Lerwick for examination in February 1917. The Navy held her for over two months.

The Navy tried enforcing the blockade with warships, but these couldn't stay at sea long enough and storms were too much for them, so the Admiralty replaced them with merchant ships. Converted passenger/cargo vessels didn't use so much coal, so they covered longer distances, and were high enough to withstand storms.

Patrol lines were between Shetland and Faroe, west of Shetland, and between Faroe and Iceland. The ships moved in zig-zag lines, changing direction to avoid submarines. They contacted each other using wireless in Morse code. They were on the lookout day and night, and challenged every ship they found.

All the armed merchantmen were equipped with guns, but the ships still resembled liners; the larger ones kept original luxurious fixtures. Ships had around six guns, with ammunition stores below decks. Naval reservists in the crew, like the Shetlanders, were seamen before the war, and this helped when investigating neutral vessels.

Armed and ready
Gunners on merchant cruiser H.M.S.
Almanzora, on patrol in the Arctic.

Armed liner at Lerwick
Merchant cruiser H.M.S. *Mantua*,
anchored at Breiwick. Liners like this
weren't seen in Lerwick in peacetime.

Liners at war

Patrolling the north
The squadron patrolled as far as Iceland;
the *Hildebrand* is anchored at Reykjavík.

Painted shell, souvenir bag
Lerwick; Cunningsburgh | 1914; 1915-1918
Painted by a crewman onboard H.M.S.
Crescent, a cruiser in the blockade force,
it shows the warship lying in Bressay
Sound. Some sailors had a sideline making
souvenir items; Leading Seaman Charlie
Tulloch, Wilhoul, bought the bag onboard
the 10th Cruiser Squadron ship *Columbella*
as a gift for a family member.
*Purchase; Donated by Charlie Simpson,
Cunningsburgh | SEA 2008.139; WAR
2014.345*

Return from patrol
Merchant cruiser H.M.S. *Orotava* entering Bustavoe.

24

Shetland crewmen
Around fifty Shetlanders
served on armed liners
such as H.M.S. *Hildebrand*.
Standing is Willie Jamieson, St
Magnus Street, Lerwick.

Ship's furniture
Foula; Dunrossness; Sandwick;
Walls | 1899-1914
Items washed ashore in western
Shetland after the armed liner
Oceanic broke up. Items were found
in several districts – the chair came
to Walls, the mirror to Bigton, and
the washstand was found at Ireland.
The sink came from the Second
Mate's cabin, and the carvings from
the state rooms.
Purchase; Chair loaned by Arnold
Goodlad, Hamnavoe | SEA 1991.212;
SEA 1992.30; SEA 2008.160

Liners at war

Armed liners in Bressay Sound
Two ships of the 10th Cruiser Squadron; nearest is the *Kildonan Castle*.

Converted for war
The merchant cruisers had been built as civilian craft, so didn't have armour to protect their hulls from enemy warships, but Britain had swept the sea of enemy warships, so guns were sufficient protection for most of what they met. This is the stern gun of the *Changuinola*.

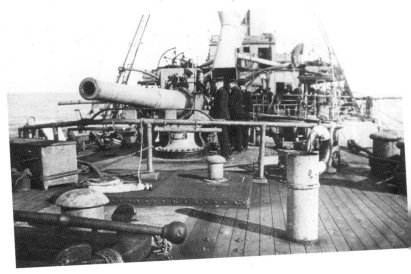

Officer class
Several officers in the 10th Cruiser
Squadron were Shetlanders. Lieutenant
Gilbert Halcrow (Valligarth, Cunningsburgh)
was a crewman on the *Armadale Castle.*

Blockade ship tableware
Foula; Delting | 1900s; 1910s
Seaman Robert Isbister, the South Biggins, saved
the teapot from H.M.S. *Oceanic* in September
1914. The cup from H.M.S. *Digby* and the jug from
H.M.S. *Gibraltar* were dropped overboard when
the ships were anchored at Bustavoe. The fork is
from a cargo ship taking supplies to the blockade
fleet; the logo is that of W. Johnston & Co.
*Purchased by support from National Fund
for Acquisitions; Donated by Billy Anderson,
Gonfirth; William Johnson, Muckle Roe | SEA
2014.63; SEA 1997.19; SEA 1997.18; WAR
1991.462*

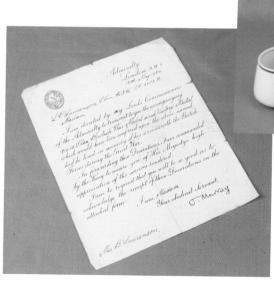

Next-of-kin letter
Nesting | 1924
Concerning Laurence Laurenson (the
Quoys), who was lost from the merchant
cruiser H.M.S. *Viknor* in the 10th Cruiser
Squadron. It states that he had been
awarded three medals for his wartime
service.
*Donated by the estate of John Laurenson,
Lerwick | WAR 2002.29*

27

When a merchant cruiser sighted a ship, she signalled it to stop; if it refused, the British fired a warning shot. Sailors were lowered in a boat, and rowed out to the neutral. This boarding party investigated the ship's documents, and did a basic search.

Ships were told to go to Lerwick or another harbour, where the authorities made a thorough examination. The boarders were armed, to make sure neutrals obeyed orders. Armed liners were at sea for three weeks, loaded supplies at Bustavoe for three days, then resumed their patrol.

At Lerwick, the Navy searched everywhere in a neutral, and if they found contraband, the Navy made the vessel go to a British port to offload the cargo. The government seized the contraband, and sometimes the ship too. After the U.S.A. joined the war, trans-Atlantic convoys replaced the 10th Cruiser Squadron, and Lerwick became Britain's convoy port. The harbour was never busier than in 1917.

Launching the boarding party
A critical part of the process was boarding the neutral vessel. This took place night or day, and in all states of sea or wind. The men in the boarding party were chosen for their exceptional seamanship, especially those from Newfoundland or Shetland.

Information highway
Edith Smith and the other typists of the Lerwick base worked around the clock to keep up with the enormous marine traffic correspondence.

Busier than ever
The blockade brought more activity to Lerwick harbour than ever before. Here we see British warships, Norwegian cargo vessels, plus Shetland and Faroese fishing craft.

Stop and search

Navy drifter
Armed drifter *Good Tidings* at Bressay Sound, with Norwegian merchant ship.

Medals
Delting | 1910s
Chief Petty Officer Jeemie Johnson (Muckle Roe) was in charge of investigating neutral ships for suspected contraband. He won the Distinguished Service Medal for saving the lives of H.M.S. *Virginian*'s boat's crew. His medals are: D.S.M., 1914-1915 Star, War Medal, Victory Medal, R.N.R. Long Service Medal.
Donated by Jessie Jamieson, Voe | CUR 6738

Sword and rifle
Lerwick | 1910s
The boarding party was armed, to make sure the neutral crew complied with orders. The officer often carried a sword and the other five sailors had rifles and bayonets.
Donated by Don Summers, Lerwick; Zetland Territorial Association, Lerwick | MIL 8195; MIL 85137

Convoy
Convoy of neutral ships assembling at Bressay Sound, 1917. The Swedish steamer *Vesterland* was sunk the day after she left Lerwick.

Revolver and belt
Unst | 1910s
Leading Seaman Charles Smith (Roselea, Baltasound) used this
equipment when boarding neutral ships at sea, and other blockade duties.
Donated by Les Smith, Lerwick | MIL 2003.227; SEA 1999.60

Storm damage
Norwegian barque
Beechbank, towed in
dismasted to Lerwic
The vessel was
seriously damaged in
a storm, and rescued
by the 10th Cruiser
Squadron.

Lerwick's sentry
The light cruiser *Brilliant* was depot and guard ship at the Lerwick base; neutral craft sent in for examination reported to her first.

Lerwick base staff
A small group of staff from the Lerwick base, at Harbour Street. While most officrs were from south, the communications, clerical and guard staff were all local.

Passage delayed
Swedish barque *Hugo Hamilton*. Shipping companies objected to
our Navy interfering with their legitimate trade. This influenced
which side neutral countries preferred. Sweden depended on
Baltic commerce, and favoured Germany.

Medals and certificates
Cunningsburgh | 1914-1919
Charlie Tulloch, Wilhoul,
served throughout the war
on the blockade. A Leading
Seaman on the *Columbella*,
he was mobilised at the
war's outbreak, and was only
discharged from the Navy in
1919. He was presented the
War Medal and Victory Medal.
*Donated by Charlie Simpson,
Cunningsburgh | WAR
2014.348*

Signals manual
Lerwick | 1910s
Signalling was vital to the blockade;
neutral ships were told to stop,
and warships communicated with
each other. Knowledge of code was
essential. This manual belonged to
Robert Johnston, Garthspool.
*Donated by Peter and Sheila Hodge,
Glasgow | SEA 1993.280*

Merchant cruiser
The Admiralty
commandeered any
suitable cargo or
passenger vessel
for the blockade
fleet. With the
size of Britain's
merchant fleet,
there were plenty
to choose from.
The *Changuinola*
is seen in fighting
mode in the 10th
Cruiser Squadron,
in wartime
camouflage.

The nerve centre
Traffic increased once convoy operations began, and hundreds of ships were processed each month by specialists at the Lerwick base, like telephonist Chrissie Kerr (the Moors, Sandwick).

A convoy departs
Convoy leaving Bressay Sound in 1917. Nearest is a Swedish steamer with deck cargo of timber.

Heavy armament
After Lerwick became Britain's convoy port in
1917, harbour defences were strengthened. This
heavy gun was installed at Aithsness, Bressay.

Ship's log and nameboards
Fair Isle | 1910s
The Danish steamer *Canadia* was wrecked whilst under escort by the 10th Cruiser Squadron with a cargo of cotton, flour and planks. The log indicated the ship's speed by recording time and distance it had run. The nameboards are from one of her lifeboats.
Donated by Alex Crawford and Simon Martin; Harry Eunson, Lerwick | SEA 74114; SEA 2008.23

The armed liners patrolled the waters west and north of Shetland. Neutral ships were determined to get through the blockade, and sometimes sneaked north around Iceland, then south along the Norwegian coast. So, the Navy used another formation to block the gap between Shetland and the westernmost point of Norway.

The 2nd Cruiser Squadron was based at Olnafirth, Delting. It consisted of armoured cruisers and converted passenger ferries called boarding steamers. They worked in pairs, with the steamer scouting ahead to increase the visibility range of the cruiser.

If the boarding steamer caught a neutral, the cruiser was onhand if any heavily-armed response was needed. The 2nd C.S. also sent in neutrals for examination, and they were most vulnerable when searching a halted ship. Their work was dangerous, and submarines attacked them.

Welcome aboard
The ships and crew of the 2nd Cruiser Squadron were
familiar visitors at Olnafirth. Besides shore visits,
local folk enjoyed occasional trips off to the ships.

A violent end
The armoured cruiser *Black Prince* was a regular visitor to Olnafirth, and crewmen
befriended local people. The district was shocked by the horrific end of the ship and all her
860 crew at the Battle of Jutland, in May 1916, when the ship was obliterated by German
battleships. The event was immortalised in Willy Stöwer's painting "Die Nachtschlacht".

Left alone
The boarding steamer *Ramsey* was sunk in August 1915 by the German armed merchant *Meteor*. John Hutchison was one of several Shetland crewmen. His widow, Flora Hutchison, is spinning at Fladdabister, Cunningsburgh, under her husband's framed medals.

Boarding stea▪
King Orry, one of the boar▪
steamers that looke▪
neutral shipping betw▪
Shetland and Norway. E▪
vessel in the flotilla w▪
converted passenger fe▪
chosen for its sp▪

The liners on patrol were just the spearhead, because they depended on supplies to keep them going. The Admiralty established their forward base in Shetland, and it chose the bays east of Swarbacks Minn, with the largest area of enclosed sheltered water. They developed everything the Navy needed.

They laid moorings for ships to anchor, and navigational markers guided the ships' paths inside the base. Coasters came with stores to replenish the depot ship, and medics cared for the sick on hospital ships. Destroyers patrolled against submarines, and minesweepers made the base approaches safe. Smaller vessels like tugs and colliers were essential to keep big ships moving.

The headquarters at Busta hosted the command and telecommunications centre, but most activity was ship-based, so jetties accommodated the launches ferrying sailors from ship to shore. The base continued until the blockade was over, but there was little left afterwards to show for this extraordinary time.

Shore leave
Crew were glad of their chance to get ashore, but the environs of north-west Shetland offered little to men accustomed to better facilities in shipping ports. The crew of the *Avenger*, here at Bustavoe in June 1917, were certainly glad to be there – their ship had just been torpedoed by the German submarine *U-69*.

Shetland mattered
Admiralty chose north-Shetland as the blockade for the Allies because is three bays – Bustavoe, firth, and Aithsvoe – all n one narrow entrance.

Leading light
Muckle Roe lighthouse was the outer navigation light that marked the entrance to Swarbacks Minn.

Fortress Shetland

The Admiral's car
Rear-Admiral William
Fawckner's chauffeur
and car at Busta.

Ditty boxes
Foula; Cunningsburgh | 1910s
The ditty box with key belonged to Peter Manson
(Blobersburn), Deck Hand in the Royal Naval
Reserve, trawler section. The other belonged to
Charlie Tulloch, Wilhoul, a Leading Seaman on the
merchant cruiser H.M.S. *Columbella*.
*Donated by Leslie Manson, Kirkcaldy; Charlie
Simpson, Cunningsburgh | SEA 7590; WAR 2014.347*

Domestic service
The Admiralty commandeered Busta,
and the housemaids continued their
duties, now waiting on Naval personnel.

The headquarters
The Navy needed few shore facilities. At Busta was the command and communications centre, and smaller boats came directly to the pier.

Sweetheart badge and Christmas card
Bressay; Aithsting | 1910s; 1917
Women often wore a badge of their sweetheart or husband's ship. This one belonged to Margaret Gray, Gunnista; H.M.S. *Brilliant* was the depot ship in Lerwick harbour. The card was sent to Chrissie Leslie, Sandsound, by a crewman on the hospital ship H.M.H.S. *Berbice*, stationed at Bustavoe.
*Purchase; Donated by Andrew Leslie, Lerwick |
WAR 1991.412; WAR 1993.154*

French officers
Lieutenant James Adie with two French officers outside Voe House. The French navy operated two of the merchant cruisers, to make a show of the blockade being an Allied effort. The British weren't impressed by their performance.

Fortress Shetland

Gun's crew base
The garage and barracks of the mobile gun and crew at Voe.

Route march
Sailors of the 2nd Cruiser Squadron marching at Voe, Delting. A Navy drifter is at the pier.

Irregular traffic
Besides the regular blockade ships' movements,
countless other warships frequented Shetland's
bays. The minelayer *Iphigenia* operated off the
west of Shetland; here she lies at Scalloway.

Hospital ship
Berbice was a hospital ship, based at Delting to cater
for sick and wounded from the 10th Cruiser Squadron.

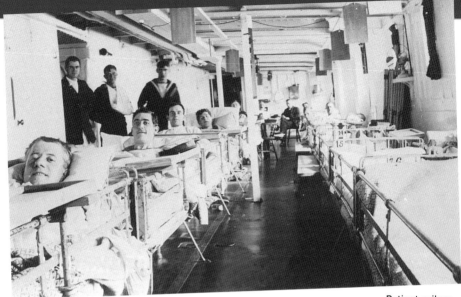

Patient sailors
Sick and injured crewmen were transferred
to the hospital ship at Bustavoe.

Officers' billet
The officers in
charge of the
Vementry gun
battery stayed
at Uyeasound,
Aithsting.

R.N.R. Medal
Northmavine | 1910s
Royal Naval Reserve Long
Service Medal, awarded to
an Henry Johnson, Heylor.
Donated by Eddie Gardiner,
Hamar | WAR 2002.109

Tugboat man
There were no big ships in the district before the war, so the Admiralty sent
tugs north to manoeuvre the scores of vessels that needed guiding every
day. Gilbert Scollay (Braeside, Delting) was a crewman on the *Flying Breeze*.

49

German submarines were the main risk to the 10th Cruiser Squadron, and the blockade ships and their base were a prime target. The Delting base was well-prepared, but the hilly geography and narrow entrance was its best defence.

A double rank of steel nets blocked the entrance against submarines, and large guns guarded the approach to the base. Sailors in watch huts scanned the coast for suspicious shipping, ready to alert defence forces. Minesweepers went out from Bustavoe every day to clear mines laid by enemy submarines.

Submarines fired torpedoes at the patrol ships, and laid mines that could sink vessels months later.

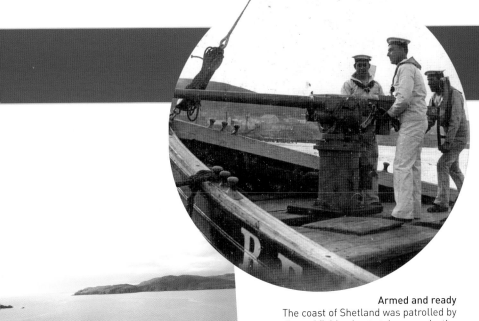

Armed and ready

The coast of Shetland was patrolled by a fleet of fishing boats taken over by the Admiralty. Converted to Navy craft, they guarded against submarines, whilst others swept enemy mines that were a huge danger to ships. These gunners are on the drifter *Ruby Gem*, at Lerwick.

ɔkout at the gate

most vulnerable part of
 base was the entrance. The
 ʋy was rightly alarmed by the
 ance of enemy submarines
 ing mines. Local sailors based
 the Braganess watch hut, near
 hsness, kept vigilant for any
 spicious sightings, and raised
 alarm by telephone.

Auxiliary patrol

Vessels of the Auxiliary Patrol, which operated against enemy submarines: a Naval steam yacht and drifters.

Armed trawler
Minesweeping trawler *Collena* at Bressay Sound in 1918.

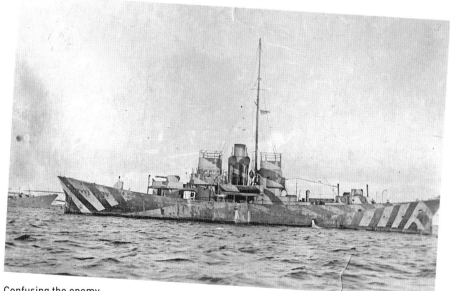

Confusing the enemy
Anti-submarine patrol gunboat designed to confuse
the enemy by disguising which end was which.

Guarding the guns
Naval rating at one of the gun emplacements at Vementry,
which were positioned to guard Swarbacks Minn.

Gunnery drill
The Voe gun's crew practising at Laxo, Lunnasting.

Under attack

First-aid practice
First-aid practice for Voe
gun's crew, at Laxo.

Line of defence
Any enemy vessel attempting a sortie
on Swarbacks Minn would have to
reckon with the battery at Vementry,
an emplacement of two naval guns
that fired a 6-inch diameter gunshell.

Watch and warn

A network of watch huts was the main part of Shetland's own wartime defences. The hut at the South Wart, Muckle Roe, occupied the most vital position of them all, because it overlooked the seaward approaches to the British blockade fleet's base, and surveyed the anchorage within. It was linked by telephone to the headquarters at Busta.

Shetland wasn't prepared to service a fighting force, because there was no Naval base before the war. The ships' crews consumed huge quantities of food, and the vessels needed refuelling on a vast scale. The Navy installed a supply network, and local firms benefited too.

Ships took supplies like clothing and tinned food to the depot ship, and the cruisers restocked each time they called. A local firm supplied beef and bread, having built a slaughterhouse and bakery for the job. The ships' steam engines devoured coal and water, so colliers were always at anchor, and the cruisers usually took two days to re-coal. The Admiralty laid a pipeline at Olnafirth to pump boiler water to the fleet.

Shops around the base did very well. Fresh food was a novelty to the crewmen, who bought meat and milk from local women, and fishermen sold their catches to the blockade ships.

Bakery staff
The Navy needed thousands of loaves every month, so the Admiralty contracted Voe firm T. M. Adie & Sons to supply. They built a bakery, which still runs to this day

ship
uiser *Gibraltar*
e depot ship at
voe, where mail
rocessed, crews
erred, and
es drawn.

k up!
ors regularly walked
Aith to the pub
esta to do some
elling of their own.

Feeding the fleet

Using our loaf
Loaves cooling on racks at
T.M. Adie & Sons' bakery,
Voe, which was established
in response to the demand
for baked goods on board
the ships of the 10th
Cruiser Squadron.

Beef for the fleet
The Adie firm
bought cattle locally,
fattened them up, and
butchered them – all
for a Navy contract.

Water tender
Besides the water station at Olna, boats fitted with water tanks came alongside Navy ships to pump water aboard directly. Peter Johnson (the North Pund, Delting) was a deck hand on one of them, the *A.C.E.S.*

Flagon
Delting | 1910s
Charlie Williamson (the Loch, Muckle Roe) got this from a 10th Cruiser Squadron vessel, and fetched paraffin from the local shop in it after the war.
Donated by Annie and Jimmy Williamson, Muckle Roe | CON 88185

59

Feeding the fleet

Trade catalogue
Delting | 1915
List of bakery machinery,
utensils and shop fittings
from the Voe bakery, which
was opened in 1915 to supply
loaf to the crewmen of the
10th Cruiser Squadron.
Donated by James Adie, Voe |
TRA 7585

Permission granted
Shetlanders were still able to fish commercially, but had to get permits from the Customs,
which detailed how far the boat could go, and when. Boats in the vicinity of the blockade base
needed an extra permit, from the Naval authorities at Busta. This one grants Alec Anderson
(Hamar, Northmavine) permission. He sold fish to the 2nd Cruiser Squadron, at Olnafirth.

The water base
The Admiralty converted the Olna whaling station
to a facility for ships to take on fresh water.

Coal
Delting | 1914-1918
Coal dredged up from
avoe. Visiting colliers
ransferred coal to the
warships during their
nchorage in this area.
ated by Ian Tait, Brae
| WAR 1996.220

Feeding the fleet

The appetite for coal
Each ship took on a thousand tons of coal when it came in, so the main duty of the blockade base was to keep the British fleet in the north supplied with coal. There were always half a dozen colliers at any time, which left and returned loaded once more, in rotation. The *Hebburn* was just one of many.

Big business
Buildings of T. M. Adie & Sons, merchants, Voe. Their business thrived during wartime.

Sheep tether and butter kit
Yell; Walls | 1900-1920
Sailors came ashore to buy sheep, eggs, socks and other local produce. Most Shetlanders had their own smallholdings and even while war conditions prevailed they were able to sell surpluses.
Donated by Bobby McLeod, Nesting; Peter Fraser, Walls | AGR 2000.47; AGR 81456

Taking on bunkers at Bustavoe
Loading coal from the collier into the ships of the blockade fleet was a huge undertaking. Most of the ship's crew was involved, shovelling coal into great baskets that were winched onto the warship, then shovelled down into the bunkers – a process called trimming.

Make yourself at home

The crewmen were glad to get ashore. Rural Shetland didn't have much to offer sailors used to busy ports, but others loved the rural scene, and the welcoming nature of the Shetlanders. Anything new broke the boredom of weeks of monotonous patrolling on the grey seas.

Sailors befriended local families, visited whenever their ship was in, and helped with farm work. Men off ships bought knitwear for their families, and wrote to their Shetland friends. Local folk attended concerts the sailors put on, and children grew up with the excitement of hundreds of ships and sailors in their midst.

Christian charities set-up facilities for music recitals, reading, and refreshments. Sailors themselves built sports pitches, fished in summer, and skied in winter. Urban dwellers in Britain experienced shortages, but Shetland was still a rural place, and islanders and their guests coped well.

Musical interlude
Bandsmen from the Royal Marines
gave performances for both sailors
and local folk at Olnafirth.

Leisurely pitch
The Navy had a football pitch and
refreshment hut at Bakka, Olnafirth.

Tea's up
Sarah Smith ran a tearoom at Roadside
Brae, selling tea and bannocks to sailors.

Mandolin man
Arthur Hodson,
a signals officer
based at Busta.

Angling
Royal Navy officers
angling at Voe.

Fourareen in Bustavoe
T. W. Scott built fourareens
for the Navy at Busta. In
distance is the recreation
hut built for the sailors of
the 10th Cruiser Squadron.

Make yourself at home

Sledging
Sailors from the cruisers at Olnafirth enjoyed winter sports, along with local folk

Peace and war
Shetland's women and children were well-used to keeping their farms going while their men were at sea. When war came, Shetlanders coped so well that they could still sell surpluses to visiting sailors.

Free labour
Shore parties of sailors helped people with their farm work. These officers are digging at Voe.

A war wedding
Not many sailors married local women, because most of the ships were only in for a few days each month, and crewmen didn't have a chance to strike up much more than a friendship. Bill Henning was a crewman on the depot ship *Gibraltar*, which was permanently based at Bustavoe, and married Joan Johnson (the North Biggins, Papa Stour).

Index